HOMETOWN
Revelations

HOMETOWN

Revelations

Legendary Folklore

How America's Cities, Towns, & States Acquired Their Names

Published and Distributed by:
DM Enterprises Inc.
1909 N. Lazy Branch Road, Suite 101
Independence, MO 64058
816-304-1334
www.dmesite.com

Cover design and artwork by Warren Utsler
Edited by Delores Cook
Inspiration & support provided by Jennifer

DISCLAIMER -The author of this book cannot guarantee the accuracy or the validity of any of the information presented. The author assumes no responsibility for errors, inaccuracies, omissions, or any inconsistency herein. Any slights of people, places, or organizations are unintentional. The intention of this book is for entertainment purposes and is not intended to be a historical work of facts. However, every effort has been made to give the most popular and accurate accounts of the origins of these names presented in this work. The real truth probably lies somewhere between the legends, the hear-say, and the reported facts.

ISBN-13: 978-0-9786987-0-6
ISBN-10: 0-9786987-0-3

LCCN: 2006905613

First Printing September 2006

Printed By:
Anchor Printing and Binding
P.O. Box 3014
Independence, MO 64055-3014
(816) 461-6757

INTRODUCTION

The names given to cities, towns, and states come from a number of sources. The origins of these names have evolved like the United States. Some of the names come from homesick settlers who wanted to remember their birthplaces. Other names originated from famous heroes and places that were known around the world. During the early history of the United States, some towns were named after new found freedoms. In the 1800's, many towns used Greek and Roman places or heroes. Native Indians were a major source of names. The early French, Spanish, and British explorers were also a major influence. Still, many other creative ways were found by our ancestors to describe their new homes. Emotional feelings or significant events were often used to name their new hometowns. Some names originated from coincidence, errors, or by sheer accident. There were even places named by the flip of a coin. Whatever the reason, we are all Americans and live in the *greatest* hometowns in the world!

Contents

I. Cities and Towns of the United States

Abilene, KS - Timothy Hershey established a stagecoach stop here in 1857. His wife, Sylvia, selected the name Abilene from Luke 3:1 in <u>The Bible</u>. The name "Abilene" means "city of the plains". Legend has it that the term "red light district" was first used here. The early railroad workers hung out their red lanterns at night for the ladies to come visit.

Akron, OH - The city was settled by the Ohio and Erie Canal Organization. The name comes from Greek origin meaning "high". In 1870, Dr. Benjamin Franklin Goodrich arrived and established a plant for making fire hose. Akron is now known as the "Rubber Capitol".

Alabaster, AL - The town was named after the limestone that was first mined in this area. The community was established in 1953.

Albany, NY - The community was named in honor of the Duke of Albany. In 1664, King Charles II gave the land to his brother James who was the Duke of Albany. Albany is the capital of New York.

Albuquerque, NM - This city gets its name from the Duke of Albuquerque, Viceroy of New Spain. The word Albuquerque comes from the Latin words "albus" and "quercus", meaning "white oak".

Allentown, PA - The city was named after William Allen. He was the early landholder and son-in-law of Alexander Hamilton. You know Alexander Hamilton. He's the one on the ten dollar bill.

Alliance, OH - The city was named because of the merging of three communities, Freedom, Mahoning and Williamsport. In 1888, a fourth was added, Mount Union. The area was founded in 1805 by Quakers from Virginia. Alliance is known as the "Carnation City".

Aloha, OR - The community's name originates from the Hawaiian word "aloha". In 1912, Robert Caples was responsible for suggesting the name. However, the locals have always pronounced it "A-low-wa".

Alton, KS - In 1870, General Hiram C. Bull and his friend Lynman T. Earl started a community here. With a flip of a coin, they decided to name their new town Bull City. Later, the General was killed by his pet elk. The General, now deceased, the town wanted a name change. There was a prominent citizen named Mrs. Clark who took it upon herself to change the town's name to Alton. This was Mrs. Clark's hometown in Illinois. She and other Kansas settlers felt that the name "Bull City" was much too vulgar.

Amarillo, TX - Coronado first explored this region in 1541. Its name is based on a variation of the Spanish word meaning "yellow". The town was founded by J.I. Berry who originally named it Oneida.

Anaheim, CA - In 1857, German settlers started a community in this area. The origin of the first part of the name comes from Santa Ana, the famous Mexican general, who lost the war to the Texans. The second part of the name originates from the German language. The word "heim" means "home".

Anchorage, AK - The city was named for the number of boats anchored at the mouth of Ship Creek. Anchorage is also known as the "City of Lights and Flowers". Every summer the community hangs out flower baskets and over 400 flower beds are planted throughout the city.

Anchorage, KY - This town is not located near a river. The word "anchorage" evolves from Captain James W. Goslee. He was a riverboat captain. When the captain retired to this area, he kept the anchor from his ship the "Matamora" in his front yard. His home was known to the local people as the "Anchorage". In 1878, after his death, the town adopted the name Anchorage in honor of him. The Captain survived many dangers in his life as a river captain, but was killed during his retirement at a railroad crossing.

Ann Arbor, MI - John Allen and Elisha Rumsey founded the town in 1824. Their wives were both named "Ann". Both men chose this name for the first part of this city's name. The last part of the city's name identified a grove of oak trees in the area. Ann Arbor is home to the University of Michigan Wolverines.

Apalachicola, FL - The community was established in 1831 and flourished. During this period, Apalachicola was the third largest port for shipping cotton. It is named after an Indian term meaning "people on the other side".

Arab, AL - This name has nothing to do with the Middle East. The first postmaster of the town decided to name the town after his son, Arad Thompson. Post Office officials mistakenly registered the town as Arab. The citizens never corrected the mishap.

Arkadelphia, AR - The town's name comes from the combination of Arkansas and "delphia", a Greek word meaning "brother".

Arkansas City, KS - Around 1870, this town was known as Walnut City. Later, it became Creswell in honor of the Postmaster General who served under President Grant. However, the name had to be changed again because of another town with that name. Kansas Senator Edmund G. Ross decided to rename the town Arkansas City. No one knows for sure how the Senator decided on this name. Senator Ross, also a railroad director, was responsible for the naming of the Atchison, Topeka, & Santa Fe Railroad. He was responsible for casting the deciding vote *not* to impeach President Andrew Johnson. Despite his many accomplishments, he died in obscurity in New Mexico.

Aspen, CO - Settled by silver prospectors in 1880, it was named for the trees located in the area. In 1891, the town was one of the nation's top silver producing industries. In 1947, Aspen Mountain opened the world's longest ski lift. Today, the city is known as a ski resort.

Astoria, OR - Astoria is the oldest settlement west of the Rocky Mountains. The town was named after John Jacob Astor. In the early 1800's, Astor owned a very successful fur company. The men who worked for Astor in this area named the town after their boss. Ironically, John Jacob never visited the town that took his name. John Jacob Astor is reported to be the first millionaire in the United States.

Atchison, KS - In 1854, Atchison became a town and was named after Senator D.R. Atchison. Atchison was a pro slavery advocate and the founders were pro slavery men. The town was home to Ameilia Earhart, the first woman to fly across the Atlantic Ocean.

Atlanta, GA - This city became the terminal of the Western & Atlantic Railroad. The railroad gave the settlement its name. The railroad came into existence in 1865 from a merger of three other railroads, the Erie & N.Y City, the Meadville, and the Franklin & Warren Railroads.

Austin, TX - The city was named in honor of Stephen Fuller Austin. He was an early Texan leader who fought against Mexico for the independence of Texas. In the early 1970's, the city became known for the renaissance and rebirth of a new type of country music.

Auxvasse, MO - T.B. Harris was the first to settle in this area around 1873. He named the area from a French term meaning "at the swamps of muddy places".

Azusa, CA - This area was settled as early as 1769. J. S. Slawson laid out the town in 1887. It was named after the Azusa land grant. The name "Azusa" originates from the Tongva Indians who lived in the area. They named the area "Asusksa-gna". This Indian term means "place of water" or "skunk". The town was incorporated in 1898.

Bad Axe, MI - The legend of this town's name comes from an early land surveyor who found a rusty old axe while platting the new town. The town was given the name "Bad Axe" from this event. Bad Axe is known as the "Hub of the Thumb".

Bagdad, AZ - There has never been a connection made with this community and the country of Iraq. The town was named from an early mining claim that was registered in the area.

Bald Knob, AR - This early settlement took its name from a local landmark in the area. There was a ridge nearby that had no trees. This ridge was an early marker for the settlers coming into the region. They were looking for the "bald knob".

Ballwin, MO - In 1826, Jefferson City became the capital of Missouri. John Ball owned 400 acres along the way of a new mail route between St. Louis and Jefferson City. John Ball wanted to capitalize on this new opportunity by forming a new town 2 miles west of the prominent town of Manchester. On February 7, 1837, the new town was named Ballshow. John Ball was very confident about the future success of his new town. He thought he would "win" from rival Manchester. Two days later, Ball amended the name of his new town to Ball<u>win</u>.

Baltimore, MD - In 1729, the prominent Carroll family helped make this an official town. It was named after its founder, Lord Baltimore. The Lord's colors of black and orange were responsible for the naming of the Baltimore oriole. Baltimore is known as the "Charm City".

Bangor, ME - The city was incorporated in 1791. Pastor Seth Noble named the town after his favorite Irish hymn. The hymn was entitled "Bangor". The city was once known as the "Queen City of the East".

Barstow, CA - The Santa Fe Railroad came to this community in 1885. The railroad named the town after its President, William Barstow Strong. Before the railroad arrived, the town was known as "Fish Pond".

Baton Rouge, LA - The origin of this name is French for "red stick". This term referred to a cypress post marking the boundary of a tribal hunting ground. The French, British and Spaniards all ruled this area at one time or another. Baton Rouge became the state capital of Louisiana in 1849.

Battle Creek, MI - The "Cereal" town was named after a skirmish between Indians and a surveying party. It is the world headquarters for the Kellogg Company.

Beaumont, TX - The traditional belief is that this city gets its name from a French term meaning "beautiful hill".

Beaver, OK - The town was named after the Beaver River which is located nearby. Needless to say, the river was named because of the beavers that lived in the river. Beaver is famous for the "World Cow Chip Throwing Championship" which is held as an annual event!

Bell Buckle, TN - The town was founded in 1856 and the name is surrounded in legend. One account believes the area was first marked by a bell and a buckle tied to a tree. Another account believes the name is a symbol signifying to early settlers that the land was good for growing crops.

Bellefontaine Neighbors, MO - In the early 1800's, land ownership to settlers in this area was made from land grants by French, Spanish, and American officials. Fort Bellefontaine was nearby and they were all neighbors. So why not name the new town, Bellefontaine Neighbors?

Belle Plaine, IA - The city's name is derived from "bell of the prairie" or "beautiful prairie". The city was established when the railroads came through in the 1850's.

Belton, MO - In 1869, Manzey Q. Ashby of Kentucky received 80 acres of land from the U.S. Government. A month later, Ashby sold the property to George W. Scott and William H. Colbern. Two years later, Scott and Colbern filed a plat calling the new town Belton. It was named for a close friend of Scott's, Captain Marcus Lindsey Belt. Both Scott and Belt had served together in the Civil War. Belt had also helped them survey the land. Famous residents of Belton have included Carrie Nation, Dale Carnegie, and the Dalton Gang.

Benton, TN - The community was established in 1840 as a county seat. It was named in honor of Missouri Senator, Thomas Hart Benton.

Bentonville, AR - The county of Benton was established in 1836. Later, the town of Bentonville was established as the county seat. Both the town and the county were named in honor of Missouri Senator, Thomas Hart Benton. This Benton guy was really popular! Bentonville is the home of Wal-Mart and J.B. Hunt.

Bethany, MO - The community was first known as Dallas but the name was not popular with the local people. Founded by John Allen of the First Christian Church in 1841, the name was changed to Bethany. The name is derived from the town of Bethlehem, the birthplace of Jesus.

Between, GA - The city was named because it is located "between" Athens and Atlanta. "Between" is *exactly* the same distance from both of these towns!

Big Island, MO - The town got its name because it was located on a big hill that was safe from the flooding water of the Black River.

Billings, MT - The city was named in honor of Frederick Billings, President of the Northern Pacific Railroad. Before the railroad, the area was only a stagecoach stop known by the name of Coulson.

Birmingham, AL - The town got its name from the English manufacturing city, Birmingham, England. Birmingham is the largest city in Alabama.

Black Jack, MO - There were three large black jack oaks that stood together providing a landmark for early pioneers traveling through this area. The oaks became a well known marker and a good stopping place to rest. These oaks were known as the "Black Jacks". Black Jack was officially christened by the Post Office in 1865.

Bliss, ID - The community was named in honor of David B. Bliss. He was an early settler to this area. Now you know why everyone here lives in *Bliss*.

Blowing Rock, NC - The community is located on a cliff overlooking a large gorge. The town's name comes from the legend that the updraft from the gorge blows back the rock one throws over the cliff.

Blue Springs, MO - Near the Little Blue River, this area was another great stop for early pioneers to rest. Its clear springs and abundance of water led to a permanent settlement called Blue Springs.

Boca Raton, FL - Many wrongfully assume the name means "Rat's Mouth". The Spanish terms "Boca" means "inlet" and "Ratones" means "mouse". However, during this time the word "mouse" was often attributed to describe a thief. The term "Thieves Inlet" or Boca Rotone was already being used on maps in the area around Miami. The community was named Boca Rotone. This was a map making mistake and the town dropped the "e" in the 1920's. The city pronounces its name "Boca Ra-tone".

Boise, ID - The community was started from the mining industry. The name "Boise" is French for "wooded". It is pronounced "Boy-See". Boise is the capital and the largest city in Idaho.

Bolivar, MO - Most settlers coming to this area in the early 1800's were from Tennessee. They named their new town after their Tennessee home. Their hometown in Tennessee was named Bolivar in honor of General Simon Bolivar, a famous South American war hero.

Bonanza, OR - The town's name comes from the Spanish word for "prosperity".

Booneville, MO - The town was founded in 1817 by Asa Morgan and Charles Lucus. They named the town in honor of Daniel Boone. Later that year, Lucus was killed in a duel by famous Missouri politician, Thomas Hart Benton.

Bootleg, TX - The origin of the name has two legends. One story suggests that it was a campground for cowboys who stopped to buy moonshine from a local still in the area. Others say that in the early 1900's, crooked realtors moved a *bootleg* school to various locations. The con men would show a small school building on the land they were selling to new prospective buyers. When the contract was signed the crooks would move the temporary school to a new location to entice other buyers. The crooks could always show that a new school was established in the community.

Boring, OR - The community was established in 1903. It was named in honor of a long time resident in the area, W. H. Boring. In the past 100 years, the town has boasted a thriving lumber industry with railroads building their tracks through this area. The citizens are still very proud of their town's name. Many businesses here use the name "Boring". There have been reports that there is a Boring Tavern with boring topless dancers!

Boston, MA - The early Puritans first settled in this area. These early pioneers often used their former hometowns to name the new settlements. Boston was named after a town in England. The city is one of the United States oldest settlements. Boston was first incorporated as a town in 1630.

Bowling Green, KY - The legend of this name occurs from the sport of bowling. It is believed that early settlers and rich lawyers that lived here played a bowling game on the grass.

Branson, MO - The town's name comes from its first Postmaster, R.S. Branson. Ever since Harold Bell Wright's novel <u>Shepherd of the Hills</u> was published, the community became a popular site for tourists. Today, Branson is considered the "Little Nashville" for country music.

Brilliant, OH - The community was named after a local glass company that operated in the area.

Buckner, MO - The town's name could have come from two sources. One source claims that it was named in honor of A.M. Buckner, a well known U.S. Senator. A.M. Buckner was very instrumental in the 1820 Missouri state constitutional convention. Others claim the town's name came from Simon Buckner, a real estate operator, who lived in the area.

Buffalo, MO - The town's name was first known as Buffalo Head. It is reported that in the early 1800's, a stake with a buffalo's head on it marked the road to this area.

Buffalo, NY - There has never been a lot of buffalo found in New York! The origin of this name has two legends. Some say it was named for nearby Buffalo Creek, which was named after an Indian who lived there. Others claim it came from the French term "beau fleuve" for "beautiful river".

Burnt Corn, AL - In 1813, an early settler Jim Cornells, returned home and found that the Creek Indians had kidnapped his wife and burned down his house. Cornell and volunteers later ambushed these Indians. This started the Indian War of 1813 and the area became known as "Burnt Corn".

Butte, MT - The early settlers named this town for a nearby peak that was located in this area. Butte is known as "the richest hill on earth". One of the biggest events each year in Butte is a motorcycle event named for Evil Knieval.

California, MO - In 1834, it was originally founded as the township of Boonesbourough. Later the name was changed to California around 1848. Legend has it that the town was named after one of its citizens, "California" Wilson. During a house raising event,

Wilson told the local residents he would buy them two gallons of whiskey if they would name the town after him. The town made good on their promise but no one knows for sure if "California" Wilson made good on his. He must have!

Callico Rock, AR - Legend says the town was named when an early explorer of the White River valley saw the beautiful limestone bluff and called it the "Calico Rocks". The explorer thought the bluff resembled the calico fabric used to make women's dresses.

Cape Girardeau, MO - The community gets its name from an early French settler by the name of Jean B. Girardot. He established a trading post here around 1725.

Carrollton, MO - The town and the county were named in honor of Charles Carroll of Carrollton, Maryland. At the time, Charles Carroll was the last surviving signer of the Declaration of Independence.

Carson City, NV - The city was named after the river located nearby. The river was named after the famous pioneer, Kit Carson. In 1858, an early pioneer by the name of Abraham Curry founded this settlement.

Casper, WY - The town is named for Casper Collins who died here fighting the Indians. He and his men were killed by the great Indian Chief, Red Cloud.

Red Cloud was never captured and continued to fight the white man until the day he died.

Cawker City, KS - The first building in this area was built in 1872. It was built by none other than Colonel E.H. Cawker, one of the town's founders. The city is well known for having the "Largest Ball of Twine" in the world.

Charlotte, NC - Early settlers named the city after Queen Charlotte of Mecklenburg. Her husband was King George III of England. Since the city was named after a queen, Charlotte has always been known as the "Queen City".

Chattanooga, TN - The origin of this name comes from an Indian word meaning "rock rising to a point". Chattanooga is located on the Tennessee River between Lookout Mountain and Signal Mountain. It is known as the "Scenic City" because of the beautiful surrounding view.

Chevy Chase, MD - The town's name has nothing to do with the famous comic. It is believed to be a reference to a battle in 1338 between England and Scotland. The Scottish word "chevauchee" means "border raid". The word "chase" means "hunting ground". Legend has it that there was also an English ballad that referred to this term.

Cheyenne, WY - Cheyenne began as a construction camp for the Union Pacific Railroad. The name's origin comes from Cheyenne Pass which was named for the Cheyenne Indians. The name "Cheyenne" is a Sioux Indian term meaning "people of a foreign language".

Chicago, IL - One source claims the town was named after an Indian word meaning "great". Other sources claim it is an Algonquian word meaning "onion place". Early settlers described the area as being covered with onions and garlic. The town was incorporated in 1833 as the Town of Chicago. Chicago is also known as the "Windy City". Some say this nickname comes from the blistering winds blowing through the downtown streets. Others claim the term comes from early politicians noted for their long winded speeches and boastfulness.

Chillicothe, MO - The town was incorporated in 1855 and is pronounced "Chil li coth ee". It is a Shawnee Indian word meaning "big town where we live" or "our big town".

China, TX - The community was first named by the Texas & New Orleans Railroad in 1860. They named their water stop China Grove because of a nearby grove of chinaberry trees. A post office opened later under the name of "China" dropping the "Grove".

Chittenango, NY - The name is an Indian term meaning "where waters divide". Frank L. Baum brought fame to the town when he published a book in 1900 called <u>The Wonderful Wizard of Oz</u>. Baum came up with "OZ" by looking at his file cabinet. The file cabinet was marked for papers O – Z.

Chugwater, WY - The name comes from an Indian term meaning "water at the place where the buffalo chugged". Legend has it that a dying Indian chief sent his son to lead the tribe on a buffalo hunt. Ahwiprie, the young warrior, devised a plan to stampede the buffalo over a cliff. When the buffalo fell from the cliffs, they made a "chugging sound" when they hit the ground. There was a stream of water nearby where this event happened.

Cincinnati, OH - The community was named after the "Society of the Cincinnati". This organization was named after the Roman General, Cincinnatus. The Society was formed to preserve the ideals of freedom and democracy. In the early 1800's, the naming of towns was in the "Classical Period". Often, the names came from Greek or Roman cities and heroes.

Clatskanie, OR - The town was named after the Tlatskanai Indians. These Indians were later known as the "Clatskanies". The word means "swift running water".

Cleveland, OH - In 1796, the city was founded and named in honor of General Moses Cleaveland. Cleveland was the chief surveyor for the Connecticut Land Company. Legend has it that an early local newspaper by the name of "The Cleaveland Advertisor", dropped the "a" from its name to accommodate the spacing of the headline banner. The city later adopted this spelling.

Climax, MI - The town was formerly known as Climax Prairie. Legend has it that the early settlers came up with the name describing their long journey. The settlers finally arrived at their new settlement and felt relief. Sorry, if this explanation disappoints you.

Coer d'Alene, ID - Visitors pronounce the name "quarter lane". It started out as a U.S. military post in 1879. The origin of this name is French. The early French fur traders called the local Indian tribe the Coer d'Alenes, meaning "heart of an awl". The French fur traders felt these Indians always "struck a hard bargain".

Coffeyville, KS - Colonel James A. Coffey established a trading post in the area. The news of his business attracted many settlers. Later, a town was laid out around the Coffey trading post. The community was named in his honor. Early on the morning of October 5, 1892, the infamous Dalton Gang met their match here.

Cole Camp, MO - The community's name comes from the actions of Captain Stephen Cole. During the early 1800's, Captain Cole and his soldiers frequently camped in this area.

Columbus, OH - The city was named in honor of Christopher Columbus who discovered America in 1492.

Colwich, KS - Colwich was founded in 1885. The Wichita & Colorado Railway had a major influence on the town at the time. The name is derived by joining the syllables "Col" and "Wich".

Conception, MO - The town's name comes from Irish Catholic railroad workers who lost their jobs in this area. With the help of a priest and others, they purchased the land. They named it Conception after Mary's "Immaculate Conception" of Jesus.

Concrete, WA - In 1871, early settlers called the town Minnehaha. Later, a post office opened and changed the name of the town to Baker in honor of a nearby river. The Washington Portland Cement Company came into the area around 1905. The company started a town named Cement City next to Baker. When the Superior Portland Cement Company opened a plant in Baker, Baker and Cement City merged and became known as Concrete!

Coon Island, MO - This was an area that stayed dry when the river flooded. During the rainy seasons, the raccoons gathered here to retreat from the high water. The area became known as Coon Island to the early settlers.

Creve Coeur, MO - The name is French for "broken heart". According to legend, an Indian princess fell in love with a fur trapper. However, the fur trapper did not return her love. The Indian princess was devastated and leaped off the cliff into the nearby lake. The lake then formed into a "broken heart". Both the city and the lake are now called Creve Coeur.

Cripple Creek, CO - Legend has it that the community was named for the cows that became lame after crossing the creek.

Cuba, MO - In 1860, G.W. Jamison moved his post office from Amanda, MO to this area. It is believed that the town was named after the Caribbean Island of Cuba. The real Cuba, at this time, was always in the headlines because its citizens were trying to get independence from Spain. During this time, many U.S. citizens sympathized with these Cuban citizens.

Cut and Shoot, TX - The origin of the name is unclear. Some feel it comes from disagreements about the steeple for the new church. Others say a boy exclaimed to a group of people that he was going to "cut around the corner and shoot through the bushes". The citizens thought about what the young boy had said and used the term for the name of their new town.

Cut Bank, MT - Lewis and Clark were the first visitors to arrive in this area that was occupied by the Blackfeet Indian Tribe. The town was named after the Cut Bank Creek which runs through this area. The creek was named "Cut Bank" because of the high banks along the creek. Cut Bank, Montana claims to be the *coldest city* in the United States.

Dallas, TX - Tradition says the city's name was in honor of Vice President George Mifflin Dallas. He was a politician from Pennsylvania and served with President James Polk. At one time, he was the mayor of Philadelphia.

Davenport, IA - In 1836, land surveys were complete and the settlement was ready to grow. Seven men gathered at Colonel George Davenport's house. Antoine LeClaire suggested that the new town be named Davenport in honor of the Colonel.

Daytona Beach, FL - In 1870, the community was laid out and platted by Mathias Day. The town was named in his honor.

Deadwood, SD - The city of Deadwood was incorporated in 1876. The city was named for the dead trees found in the nearby canyon. Famous residents have included Wild Bill Hickock, Calamity Jane, and Wyatt Earp.

Dearborn, MI - The city was named after Pamela Augusta Dearborn. She was the daughter of Revolutionary War hero, General Henry Dearborn.

Defiance, MO - Two farm communities competed with each other for the services of the railroad coming into the area. Each group won a train stop. The first named its community Matson. The other community chose Defiance. The people of Defiance felt that it had defied the odds in getting the railroad services it wanted as well as defying Matson its rival.

Delaware Water Gap, PA - This town is close to the Pennsylvania and New Jersey border. In this area, there is a gap where the Delaware River flows between Mount Tammany and Mount Minsi. The town is truly named from the description of this landmark.

Denver, CO - The community was named in honor of General James W. Denver, Governor of the Kansas Territory. General Denver was also a California politician and a military officer who fought in the Mexican-American War.

Deposit, NY - Legend claims the name comes from lumber which early settlers *deposited* in the area. During these times, early settlers gathered large amounts of lumber and stacked it near the river banks. When the river would rise from the rain, the lumber was easier to load onto ships to take to other locations downstream.

Derby, KS - The town was first named El Paso, KS in 1871. In 1879, the Santa Fe Railway continued to have confusion delivering the mail to El Paso, KS and El Paso, TX. The railroad decided to rename the Kansas community Derby, in honor of one of their officials. The citizens accepted this decision and the town was known as Derby.

Des Moines, IA - Some people believe the name is an Indian term meaning "river of the mounds". This term refers to the Indian burial grounds that were found near the river. Other historians feel the name comes from the Monks who lived in the area. They lived in huts at the mouth of the Des Moines River. The early French explorers referred to the area as "La Riviere des Moines". Des Moines is a variation of this term shown on early maps of the area.

Detroit, MI - The community was settled along the Detroit River. The river in this area narrows. Detroit is a variation of a French word meaning "the narrows".

Dodge City, KS - The town was named in honor of Major General Grenville M. Dodge. Fort Dodge was also named after this general. General Dodge became famous in the Civil War and was later considered to be the best railroad builder in the nation. Wyatt Earp and Bat Masterson were once law officers here.

Downs, KS - In 1854, Major William F. Downs brought the Central Railroad to this area. The town was named in his honor.

Dover, DE - The community took its name from a port city in England. Dover is the capital of Delaware.

Drain, OR - The town was named in honor of Charles C. Drain who donated his land for the town. Drain had a huge house in town known as the Drain Castle.

Dubuque, IA - The city was named in honor of an early settler, Julian Dubuque. Dubuque got permission from the Fox Indians to mine the area. He became a very good friend to the tribe and later became one of their chiefs. The Fox Indians felt so loyal to him they even provided a grave site for him overlooking his town.

Durango, CO - The community's name comes from a Basque word "urango" meaning "water town".

Dwarf, KY - The community was named after Jeremiah Combs who lived in this area. Jeremiah was known to the citizens as "Short Jerry".

Eagleville, TN - In 1832, the town was originally known as Manchester but the Post Office notified the community that there was already another town using that name. Around this time, a very large eagle was killed in this area. The citizens decided to use this event to name their new town and post office.

Early, TX - The community was started in the 1920's and was named in honor of an attorney, Walter U. Early.

Elkader, IA - In 1836, the first permanent residents arrived. The town was named in honor of Abdal Kader, a young Algerian hero who led his people against the French between 1830 and 1847.

El Paso, TX - In 1581, the Spanish Conquistadores found their way across the Rio Grande River. The pass was named "El Paso", the Spanish term meaning "the pass". In 1598, Don Juan de Onate colonized the area and officially named it El Paso.

Embarrass, WI - The town was named after the nearby Embarrass River. The river's name comes from a French word meaning "impede" or "entangle". Floating logs often got stuck in this part of the river.

Eminence, MO - The town was named in honor of the Kentucky hometown of Judge George "Peg Leg" Shannon. "Peg Leg" was a member of the Lewis and Clark Expedition.

Eureka, MO - In 1853, the Missouri Pacific Railroad was building its tracks through the city of Franklin, MO. Franklin's rocky ground and little dirt made the railroad builder's life difficult. After the rail was completed in Franklin, the workers looked westward and saw level land and no rocks ahead. They cried out "Eureka" which in Greek means, "I've found it"! The next town was named Eureka!

Fairplay, CO - The legend of this name says that early settlers named the town to guarantee that all citizens would be treated equal.

Fargo, ND - The city was named after William G. Fargo, Director of the Northern Pacific Railway. He was also the founder of American Express and the Wells-Fargo Express.

Flagstaff, AZ - In 1876, settlers in the area made a pine tree into a flagpole. It was the 100th anniversary of the Declaration of Independence. After hanging the U.S. flag on their newly made flagpole, the community decided on the name of Flagstaff.

Flippin, AR - In 1820, Thomas J. Flippin took his family from Hopkins County, Kentucky and moved into this area. A traveling salesman called the place Goatville, but the residents did not like its connotations. They thought it should be called Flippin Barrens in honor of Flippin and because there were very few trees in the area. The Post Office only agreed upon the name of Flippin.

Flushing, NY - The community was established by the Dutch in the early 1600's. The name is an English translation of "Vlissingen". Vlissingen is a harbor city in the Netherlands.

Folkston, GA - The community was established by the Savannah, Florida & Western Railroad around 1880. The town was built because the railroad needed a station in this area. The community was first known as "the station" but was later named "Folkston" in honor of Dr. William B. Folks. Folkston is famous for the "Folkston Funnel". All the railroads intersect here because it's the only way a train can enter the state of Florida. The town has built a platform for visiting and local train watchers. Over 40 different trains pass through the town daily!

Fond Du Lac, WI - The word comes from the French words meaning "end of the lake". The city is located near Lake Winnebago.

French Lick, IN - The name has nothing to do with French kisses. The French built a fort here and the name comes from the salt springs located in the area. It is the hometown of Larry Byrd, the famous basketball player.

Fresno, CA - The city's name is Spanish for "ash tree". Fresno is the sixth largest city in California.

Friend, NE - The community was named in honor of Charles E. Friend who donated his land for the town.

Gallup, NM - The name does not come from the many horses that galloped through New Mexico. The Atlantic & Pacific Railroad started a railhead here in 1881. The community was named after the railroad's pay master, David L. Gallup.

Garden City, KS - The Fultons ran the Occidental Hotel in 1878 and were one of the first to settle in the area. Mrs. Fulton had a beautiful garden near the hotel. Her unusual flowers were new to this part of the country. The drifters and railroad workers admired her garden so much that they convinced her to name the town "Garden City".

Gas, KS - E.K. Taylor the founder, proclaimed that his town was "founded upon natural resources that would erect and maintain a city as solid as the Rock of Gilbraltar". E. K. wanted the town to be called Gas

City, but reluctantly accepted the Post Office's decision to drop the word "city".

Gnadenhutten, OH - Germans brought 90 Christian Indians to settle in this area in the late 1700's. They named the settlement "Gnadenhutten" which means "huts of grace". The Indians were later massacred. In 1798, John Heckenweldon built the first house and started a new community.

Gnaw Bone, IN - The town was originally named Narbonne, after a town in France. When the English settlers migrated to this area, they translated the name to what they had heard.

Grain Valley, MO - It was easy to name this town. In September of 1878, the citizens looked out and saw the abundance of grain in the valley.

Grand Island, NE - The city was established on an island formed from the Platte River. Grand Island is the third largest city in Nebraska.

Grand Rapids, MI - Once a fur trading and lumber center, the town was named for its swift rapids in the river.

Green Bay, WI - The early French settlers called it La Baie Verte or "Green Bay". The city is often referred to as "Titletown" because of the success of

Vince Lombardi and the Green Bay Packers football team.

Gunnison, CO - The community was named in honor of John W. Gunnison. Gunnison was a famous surveyor who was killed by Indians here while doing his job.

Hackensack, NJ - The community was established in 1647. The community's name comes from an Indian term meaning "mouth of the river".

Happy, TX - Legend says that the town was first known as Happy Draw. It is believed that early cowboys were extremely *happy* to find water here for themselves and their horses.

Harrisonville, MO - In 1837, the town was established as a county seat. It was named in honor of Albert G. Harrison, one of the first U.S. Congressmen elected from the state of Missouri. Col. H.W. Younger was the mayor in 1859. The mayor's son became outlaw Cole Younger.

Hartford, CT - The community was named after Hartford, England. Hartford is the capital of Connecticut.

Hays, KS - In 1886, General Hancock named the fort and the town in honor of General Alexander Hays.

General Hays was killed in 1864 during the Civil War at "The Battle of the Wilderness".

Hazard, KY - The city was founded in 1820. It was named in honor of Commodore Oliver Hazard Perry. Perry was a Navy hero from the War of 1812.

Helena, MT - The town was named after Helena, Minnesota. Helena, MN was named in honor of Helen of Troy. Helena is the capital of Montana.

Hell, MI - George Reeves first settled this community in 1838. He built a general store and a mill. George also ran a whiskey still and got some of his neighbors in trouble. Their wives would often exclaim that "they went to Hell" (referring to George's still) where they would hang out and drink with George. In 1841, the State of Michigan asked George what he wanted to call his town. George exclaimed "Call it Hell, everyone else does". In October of 1841, Hell became the official name.

Herculaneum, MO - Moses Austin founded the town in 1808. It became a shipping point for the lead smelting operations in the area. Austin had a great imagination. He envisioned that the smoke emitting from the lead plants resembled Mt. Vesuvius and the limestone in the area was a Roman amphitheater. He named the town in memory of an ancient Roman town that was destroyed by the lava from Mt. Vesuvius.

Hermann, MO - A German society in Philadelphia planned and named the city for their migrating German pioneers who were headed west. They wanted their fellow Germans to have a city in the far west that was German in every tradition. Hermann, Missouri is very famous for its vintage wine started by these early German settlers.

Hershey, PA - Not only did Milton S. Hershey build a chocolate dynasty here, he also built a town for his workers. The town was named in his honor.

Hicksville, OH - Henry W. Hicks was a wealthy shipping merchant from New York. In 1820, Ohio started selling land for $1.25 an acre! Hicks formed a land company and started purchasing land in Ohio. In 1839, Hicksville was platted and a town was established. In the early 1900's, the town was considered to be one of the best places to live in Ohio. However, you could be fined $5.00 for spitting on the sidewalk!

Higginsville, MO - In 1869, the city was founded by Harvey Higgins. Higgins donated his land to build the town.

Hilliard, MO - The name comes from the yard where George Hill supplied wood for the steam engines on the Iron Mountain Railroad. Hill's Yard became a fuel stop for the trains. When the Post office came to town the name was changed to Hilliard, a more sophisticated name.

Hog Eye, AR - The name has nothing to do with the animal. In the 1800's, a small settlement located in a hollow or valley was often referred to as a *Hog Eye*. Missouri and Texas had a lot of little towns by this name but they all vanished or changed their names. The people of this town in Arkansas decided to keep the name.

Ho-Ho-Kus, NJ - The town was formed in 1908. It was first known as the Borough of Orvil. The community wanted to name itself after the County of Hohokus. To avoid confusion, the Borough Council added hyphens and capitalizations to distinguish the town from the county.

Hollywood, CA - In the 1880s, Harvey Henderson Wilcox, a wealthy real estate businessman from Topeka, Kansas moved here with is wife, Daeida. Wilcox let his wife name his new town. Daeida Wilcox had met a woman on a train trip and the woman spoke of her home in Ohio named Hollywood. Daeida loved the name so much that she decided to use it for the name of her new town.

Holyrood, KS - In 1886, Hollyrood was developed after the Santa Fe Railroad came through this area. It was named after a city in Canada by the name of

Hollyrood with two "L"s. One day, the Kansas winds blew one of the "L"s off of the depot sign. The sign was never repaired and the shorter name Holyrood became official in 1898.

Hominy, OK - The town was originally named Harmony. Legend has it that "Hominy" became the name because of incorrect mispronunciation and spelling. It was common for the different dialects of people to confuse the issue.

Honolulu, HI - The city's name is Hawaiian for "sheltered harbor". Honolulu is the capital of Hawaii.

Hope, AR - The origin of this town's name comes from railroad history. It was named after a railroad director's daughter, Hope Loughborough. Hope, Arkansas was the boyhood home of President Bill Clinton.

Houston, TX - Sam Houston became the first president of Texas. In 1836, he defeated Santa Ana and Texas became independent from Mexico. In the same year, Houston became the capital of Texas and was named in his honor.

Hughesville, MO - The town was founded by Reese Hughes, a prominent landowner and lawyer in this area. He first laid out the community in 1878. Reese opened one of the town's first stores. The town became the largest shipping point for cattle between Kansas City and St. Louis. These are facts and are not legends about this community. I am married to Reese's great, great granddaughter!

Humansville, MO - The community was founded by a real live human! His name was James G. Human.

Huntsville, AL - The city was named after John Hunt, the first settler of the land. However, Hunt did not properly register his claim and lost his land. The area was then purchased by Leroy Pope who named the town Twickenham. This name was chosen to honor a distant relative's hometown in England. The War of 1812 caused the town's name to become Huntsville. The citizens wanted nothing to do with England!

Hurricane, UT - In the 1800's, Erastus Snow was returning home when a large gust of wind swept off the top of his buggy. He exclaimed that the experience was like "going through a hurricane"!

Hurt, VA - This is not a painful story. The community was named in honor of Major John L. Hurt. During the Civil War, Major Hurt was in charge of the gun powder production that was being produced in this area.

Iconium, MO - The town is correctly named. The small little town is located out of the way of any major highway or community. Iconium was a name used to describe a Turkish oasis in the desert. The name "Iconium" is pronounced "I-Cone-ni-um".

Independence, MO - In the early 1800's, this community chose its name in honor of the Declaration of Independence. During this time, many towns chose names that described the new found freedom of the United States. Independence is called the "City of Trails" because this was the starting point for the Santa Fe, Oregon, and California Trails. A favorite legend of the town occurred sometime in the late 1850's. A young man was caught up in a barroom brawl late on a Saturday night. He went wild and began punching and knocking out the patrons who had started the fight. The bystanders, who witnessed the fight, gave the young man the nickname of "Wild Bill". The nickname stuck and from that day forward, the young man was known as "Wild Bill" Hickock.

Intercourse, PA - The town was originally founded in 1754. It was known as Cross Keys after a tavern in the area. There are several unsubstantiated versions of the origin of the name "Intercourse". Some say the name described the long entrance to an old race track east of town. This stretch of road was first known as the "Entercourse". By 1814, the name evolved into Intercourse. Another explanation suggests that the name comes from two well known traveled roads that crossed in the middle of the town. Today, the town is a well-known Amish settlement.

Itta Bend, MS - This town was named after a Choctaw Indian term meaning "camp together". The community is home to Mississippi Valley State College and the birthplace of blues guitarist, B.B. King.

Jackson, MS - Long before the Civil War, the early settlers admired the Union. They named their town after Major General Andrew Jackson, who later became the seventh President of the United States. Jackson is the capital of Mississippi.

Jacksonville, FL - This city was also named in honor of President Andrew Jackson. In 1791, the settlement was known as Cow Ford.

Jamesport, MO - It is unclear of the origin of this town's name. Some feel that it was named for either the first Postmaster, James Gililan or for James Callison, who was Gililan's brother-in-law. Callison was a local landowner. Another account says the town was named in honor of Dr. James T. Allen who surveyed the town's site.

Jefferson City, MO - The city is named in honor of President Thomas Jefferson. Jefferson City became the capital of Missouri in 1821. Originally, St. Charles was the capital.

Jekyll Island, GA - The land was purchased in 1886 by the Jekyll Island Club. The Jekyll Island Club was an exclusive group of millionaires which included the Rockefellers, Morgans, Astors and the Vanderbilts. The city became the winter home for these elites.

Jetmore, KS - Founded in 1879, this town was named after a Topeka lawyer who helped the town become the county seat of Hodgeman County. The town was incorporated in 1887.

Jewell, KS - Both the county and the town were named for Colonel Lewis R. Jewell. He was considered a very gallant officer in the Civil War. The colonel settled near Ft. Scott, KS but never visited the town which bears his name.

Joplin, MO - In July of 1871, John C. Cox laid out a town in this area. Cox chose the name of Joplin in honor of his friend, Reverend Harris G. Joplin. Joplin thrived as a city due to its richness in ore and mining opportunities.

Juneau, AK - Joseph Juneau, an early prospector from Canada, found gold here. At first, the town was not named after him. Joseph had to spend some of his gold on bribes to the local miners so they would vote for the name change. The city of Juneau is the capital of Alaska.

Kalamazoo, MI - The name of this community comes from an Indian term "kalamazoo" meaning "otter trail".

Kankakee, IL - The community was named after the Kankakee River which was named after an Indian term meaning "swamp land".

Kansas City, MO - In 1829, Francois Chouteau called it the village of Kansa. Kansa was a tribe of Indians that lived in the area. Later in 1838, John Calvin McCoy and his investors formed the Town of Kansas. Many names were considered, such as Rabbitsville and Possum-trot but the group chose the name Town of Kansas. Later in 1853, the name was changed to the City of Kansas. In 1889, the official name became Kansas City. Kansas City is also known as the "City of Fountains". The community has more water fountains than any other in the United States.

Kearney, MO - The origin of this name is clouded in controversy. Some feel it was named in honor of General S.W. Kearney who led Missouri soldiers into the Mexican War of 1846. Others feel it was named for Charles E. Kearney who was a railroad official.

Keokuk, IA - This community was named after the Sauk Fox Indian Chief, Keokuk. The Indian word "keokuk" means "watchful fox".

Kill Devil's Hill, NC - There are two legends that surround this town's name. In the 1700's, it was reported that the rum which was drunk in the area was so bad that they called it "Kill Devil". Another version says that a ship, carrying Kill Devil rum, wrecked upon the hills in the area.

Kirksville, MO - Legend has it that Jesse Kirk, an early settler, pledged free whiskey and dinner for the surveyors if they named the community for him. I guess Jessie kept his promise!

Knob Knoster, MO - The town was named after a large hill in the area that was referred to as a knob. The word "knoster" is Latin for "our".

Knoxville, TN - The community was named after General Henry Knox, a famous Revolutionary War hero. He fought in the "Battle of Bunker Hill". Famous country music entertainers, Kenny Chesney and Chet Atkins started their careers here.

Lamoni, IA - The origin of this name comes from a king in the Mormon Bible. Lamoni is home to Graceland College.

Lansing, MI - In 1842, John North founded the community. North named his town after his hometown in New York. Lansing is the capital of Michigan.

Laramie, WY - The town is named for an early French fur trapper. His name was Jaque La Ramee. The origin of the name is from the combination of the "La" and "Ramee".

Laredo, TX - Early pioneers settled near the river in this area. A town began to emerge in 1755. The origin of the name comes from a town in Spain.

Las Vegas, NV - This doesn't make sense but the city's name is Spanish for "the meadows". In 1942, Bugsy Siegel opened the Flamingo Casino. Today, Las Vegas is considered the "Gambling Capital" of the world.

Leavenworth, KS - In 1827, Colonel Henry H. Leavenworth established the site for military purposes. The fort and the town are named in his honor.

Lebanon, TN - The town was founded in 1802. The early settlers named their new community "Lebanon" because of the many cedar trees found in the area. The name is in reference to "Mount Lebanon" in The Bible. Cedar trees were highly valued and believed to have spiritual qualities to both the biblical people and these early settlers in Tennessee. Today, Lebanon is the corporate headquarters for Cracker Barrel Old Country Stores.

Lebo, KS - The town was named in honor of one of the earliest settlers in the region, Josiah Leabo. Later, the name was shortened to Lebo.

Lee's Summit, MO - Originally, the town was known as Strother. In 1868, the name was changed to the Town of Lee's Summit. The "Summit" portion is believed to have come from the fact that the town's elevation is the highest point on the railroad between Kansas City and St. Louis. However, the "Lee's" part of the name has two versions. One theory suggests that it was named after General Robert E. Lee. Many of the citizens living here at the time were southern sympathizers. Others believe the "Lee's" came about in honor of an early settler, Dr. Pleasant Lea. They say the discrepancy in the name of "Lea" was due to poor spelling by railroad sign painters.

Liberal, KS - The town was founded in 1888. Water was very scarce in the 1880's but S.S. Rogers had dug a well on his homestead and offered free water to the visitors and their livestock that passed through the area. This was unusual because water was not free. The surprised visitors would comment to Rogers that "this was mighty *liberal* of you". The name caught on and was known to travelers as Liberal. Kansas has always been considered a conservative state.

Licking, MO - In 1826, a large salt lick was discovered in the area. The town was first known as "The Lick". Later in 1857, when the town was platted, the citizens and the Post Office preferred the name Licking.

Little Flock, AR - The legend of the name says it comes from a Biblical phrase in The Bible "Fear not, little flock".

Little Rock, AR - The early settlers gave the community its name from the little rock along the river banks. Little Rock is the capital of Arkansas.

London, KY - You are right! It was named after London, England. However, did you know it was the home of Colonel Harland Sanders, founder of Kentucky Fried Chicken?

Loogootee, IN - Natural gas was discovered here in 1899. The community's name combines Lowe, the first engineer to drive a train through town, with Gootee, who was the landowner of the town.

Looneyville, TX - This is not a crazy name at all. The town was named in honor of John Looney. Looney opened the first store in this area around

1870. He established a post office in his store in 1874.

Los Angeles, CA - Originally settled by the Spanish, the name given to this town was "Reina de los Angeles" or "Queen of the Angels".

Louisville, KY - The community was named for French King Louis XVI. The French people later found King Louis guilty of treason. He and his wife, Marie Antoinette, were both be-headed. Residents pronounce the city's name as "Lu-a-vull". The city is world renowned for the Kentucky Derby.

Lovelady, TX - Sorry, there is no lady responsible for the name. In 1872, the Houston & Great Northern Railroad bought the land from an early settler by the name of Cyrus Lovelady. The town was named in his honor.

Lubbock, TX - The city is named after Thomas S. Lubbock who was a Texas Ranger. His influential brother was Francis R. Lubbock, Governor of Texas during the Civil War.

Luck, WI - The most popular legend for the town's name is from the wagon trains that traveled through this area in the 1850's. If passengers could make it to this site from St. Croix Falls by nightfall, they considered that they were in luck!

Luckenbach, TX - The town was named by its first Postmaster, Mrs. Albert Luckenbach. Hondo Crouch bought the town in 1971 and invited Willie Nelson and the boys to visit. The rest is history.

Lyons, KS - The name of this town comes from the landowner where the town was established. William Matthewson dug a well in the area. Later, William Matthewson was known as "Buffalo Bill Cody".

Macon, GA - The town was named in honor of Nathaniel Macon. Macon fought in the Revolutionary War and was a famous congressman and senator from North Carolina.

Madison, WI - The community was named after President James Madison. It became the capital of Wisconsin in 1836.

Malta Bend, MO - In 1841, a steamboat named the "Malta" sank in the river bend near this area. The town decided on the name because of this historical event and landmark.

Manhattan, KS - On Valentine's Day in 1857, Manhattan Kansas became an official town. The Cincinnati Company was responsible for its name. Their goal was to start a town in the west by the name of Manhattan. They thought their new city was going to become a second Manhattan, New York. The

Kansas community is still considered the "Little Apple".

Manhattan, NY - When the early Dutch arrived, they named the area after the Indian tribe that lived here. The word translates as "small island" or "hilly island". In 1626, the Indians sold Manhattan to Peter Minuit for $24.00!

Marceline, MO - In 1887, the Santa Fe Railroad built a terminal here. This location was chosen and the town was platted. Marceline was chosen as the name at the request of one of the railroad directors. His wife's name was Marcelina and with a vowel change, Marceline became the new name for the railroad city. Recent findings however, reveal that the name could have come from an early French settler by the name of Marceline Silvadon. Records show that Marceline was an early landowner in the area. Marceline was the boyhood home of Walt Disney.

Marshall, MO - This community was established in 1839 and was named by the county court in honor of U.S. Supreme Court Justice, John Marshall.

McPherson, KS - This town was named after the famous General James "Birdseye" McPherson. General McPherson led the Army of the Tennessee in the Civil War. He was considered one of General Sherman's best generals. However, "Birdseye" met his match and was killed in 1864. A life-size bronze statue of the general on his horse was dedicated to the town in 1917.

Memphis, TN - The name was chosen after the city in Egypt. Memphis is famous for blues music and is the largest city in Tennessee.

Mesa, AZ - This name was chosen because the community was built on a plateau overlooking a valley.

Miami, FL - One account says that the city got its name from an Indian term meaning "very large". Another theory says that the name is an Indian term meaning "sweet water". Miami is often referred to as the "Gateway to America".

Middlesex, NJ - No love stories are associated with this name. The early settlers named their town in honor of Middlesex, England. The name Middlesex refers to the "Middle Saxons", a group of people who lived in early England.

Milwaukee, WI - This city gets its name from an Indian term that means "gathering place by the river", "good land" or "there is a good point".

Minneapolis, MN - The name combines a Sioux Indian term and a Greek word. The Indian word means "water" and the Greek word means "city". Minneapolis is the capital of Minnesota.

Mobile, AL - The origin of this name comes from an Indian tribe. The Spanish called this area Mauvila. Through the years, the name evolved into Mobile. What an evolution!

Monkeys Eyebrow, KY - Legend has it that if you stand at the top of the hill and look down, the town appears to look like the eyebrow of a monkey. The problem with this legend is what does a monkey's eyebrow look like?

Montpelier, VT - The city was established as the capital of Vermont in 1805. The community gets its name from the same town in France.

Murfreesboro, TN - The town was originally named Cannonsburgh in 1811. However, the site of the new community was owned by Captain William Lytle. The Captain petitioned the legislature to change the name. He wanted the town to be called Murfreesborough in memory of his friend, Colonel Hardy Murfree. In 1817, the legislature honored the Captain's request but changed the name to Murfreesboro.

Muscle Shoals, AL - The name has nothing to do with being physically fit. The community is located on the Tennessee River. During early times, the rapid waters in the river were often referred to as "mussel shoals". The origin of the city's name is a variation of this term.

Muskogee, OK - The town was named in honor of the Muskogee Indians who first lived in this area. Merle was not originally from Muskogee!

Nags Head, NC - Legend has it that early pirates were responsible for the name. The pirates would hang a lantern around a horse's (nag) head and walk up and down the beach on a stormy night. When the horse walked the light resembled another ship. This behavior lured unsuspecting ships toward the shoreline. The pirates were then able to rob and pillage the innocent ship.

Nashville, TN - The city was named in honor of Revolutionary War hero General Francis Nash. In 1777, General Nash was mortally wounded at the "Battle of Germantown". The city became a thriving river port in 1818.

Natchitoches, LA - The town has a long history. Louis Juchereau de St. Denis came here in 1714 to build a fort. It was near an Indian tribe called the "Natchitoches".

Needles, CA - The community gets its name from the description early settlers gave to the peaks along the Arizona side of the Colorado River.

Neptune City, NJ - The town was incorporated in 1881. It was named after the Roman God. Most of the town was later swallowed up by another city. Oddly enough, the town that took away the land is named "Avon by the Sea".

Newark, NJ - One source says the city was named after a town in England. It was first founded by the Puritans. The other legend says the name stems from The Bible meaning "New Ark".

New Madrid, MO - Colonel George Morgan acquired a land grant in 1786 from the Spanish Governor Esteban R. Miro. Because of the generosity from the governor, Morgan named his new town in honor of the capital of Spain.

New Orleans, LA - The "Crescent City" originates from the French. It was named after the town in France and for the Duke of Orleans.

New York, NY - "The Big Apple" got its name from York, England and the Duke of York. There are various accounts why New York is called the "Big Apple". It could have come from the apple vendors during the Depression. Others say it was named after a famous Harlem jazz club. Still others profess it was named the "Big Apple" from a well known dance craze in the 1930's. None of these accounts have ever been substantiated.

Niceville, FL - Originally, the community was known as Boggy Bayou. James E. Plew promoted the area by bringing people from Chicago to visit. Everyone loved the beautiful boggy bayou, the golf course, and the wonderful climate. It was definitely a *nice* place to live. In 1938, the citizens decided to name it Niceville.

Nicodemus, KS - In July of 1877, a black community was established by former slaves coming from Kentucky. They decided to name their new town based on the story from The Bible.

Nimrod, MN - The community was a booming lumber town in the early 1900's. Today, you may find only a gas station in this area. The town was named after a Mesopotamian King mentioned in The Bible. Others say that the word "nimrod" means "hunter".

Nixa, MO - Nicholas A. Inman was an active leader here in 1852. He was a blacksmith that had moved here from Tennessee. As the community grew and more businesses opened, a town meeting was held to choose a name. It was suggested that the town should be named "Inman" because of the years of service that Nicholas had given to the community. Others suggested the term "nix", because the community was nothing but a crossroad. During the meeting, an "a" was added to the "nix" in honor of Inman and the final name for the town became Nixa.

Nome, AK - Legend has it that the name comes from poor map making errors. The original notation on the map was <u>name?</u> Map makers made an error and misinterpreted the notation as "Nome". This error became the new name for this town.

Norfolk, VA - Early English settlers named the town after a county in England. Norfolk is one of the oldest communities in the United States. The city is also a strategic naval port.

Oakland, CA - The city was named after the many evergreen oak trees that grew in this area.

Ogallala, NE - The town was named for the band of Oglala Sioux Indians. The early settlers changed the spelling.

Omaha, NE - The city was named in honor of the Omaha Indians. Omaha is home to the largest population of millionaires in the United States.

Ordinary, VA - The name comes from a term that was used in the late 1700's to describe a general store that was combined with an inn.

Orlando, FL - The city was named in honor of Orlando Reeves. Orlando Reeves was a soldier killed here by the Indians. Orlando is headquarters to Disney World.

Osceola, MO - The community was named in honor of famous Seminole Chief, Osceola. The chief was a fierce warrior who accepted a peace treaty by the U.S. but was later deceived and put in prison where he died.

Ottumwa, IA - The city was named from an Indian term meaning "swift" or "rapid water".

Ozone, AR - There is mystery and speculation in this town's name. As German immigrants settled in Arkansas, they often chose names from their hometowns. In 1837, German scientist Christian Schonbein discovered *ozone*. It is believed the early immigrants that settled here chose the name "ozone" in his honor.

Paducah, KY - George Rogers Clark first picked the area for a new settlement. In 1821, his brother named the town after a Chickasaw Indian Chief named Paduke. Others say the name "Paducah" comes from a group of Comanche Indians who called themselves the Padoucas.

Pall Mall, TN - The town was named in honor of the city in England and not for the cigarettes!

Paradise, PA - The community was established in 1804. Legend has it that Joshua Scott, a local map maker, was responsible for the name of this town. When he looked at the beautiful scenery that surrounded him, Scott exclaimed, "This place seems like *paradise*"! The citizens agreed and named their town after Scott's suggestion.

Paris, TN - The town was established in 1823. The famous French Revolutionary War hero, Lafayette, visited this area many times. The citizens named their town in honor of Lafayette's capital in France. The community is known for the "World's Biggest Fish Fry" which happens annually.

Parrott, GA - The Creek Indians first settled in the area. Their village was known as Chenuba. In 1889, the town was established and the name was changed to Parrott. It was named in honor of John Lawson Parrott who donated his land to start the town.

Pasadena, CA - The origin of this name comes from an Indian term meaning "valley" or "crown of the valley". The *Rose Parade* is a New Year's event.

Pawtucket, RI - The community was named after an Indian term meaning "river fall". It is also the birth place of America's most popular potato, MR. POTATO HEAD!

Peculiar, MO - The name of this town is surrounded in legend. Some believe a spiritualist having a *peculiar* vision of this area named the town after his experience. Others believe the name comes from a frustrated postmaster in town. All of the names he suggested to the Post Office kept getting rejected. The Post Office suggested "choose a name that is peculiar". The postmaster followed the government's instructions and named the town Peculiar.

Pella, IA - The community's name is derived from a Hebrew term meaning "city of refuge". Today, the city is very Dutch and is noted for tulips.

Philadelphia, PA - William Penn planned this community. The name is Greek for "brotherly love". The Indians first occupied this area. They called the town Shackamaxon. At one time, Philadelphia was the largest town in North America.

Phoenix, AZ - The early pioneers built their new settlement on the site of a former village. They called it Phoenix, referring to the fabled bird that rose from its ashes.

Pierre, SD - The city was named for Pierre Choteau Jr. of the American Fur Company. Pierre has been the capital of South Dakota since 1889.

Pigeon Forge, TN - The name comes from two sources. In the late 1700's there were many carrier pigeons in the area. The river nearby became known as "Pigeon River". In 1820, Isaac Love established a furnace and an iron forge in this area. The town's name comes from the "Pigeon" river and the "Forge" from Love's operation.

Pilot Grove, MO - The town gets its name from a landmark in the area. In the 1820's, early settlers used a grove of trees in the area to guide or pilot their way across the prairie. Later, a community was started here.

Pittsburg, PA - The community was named in honor of William Pitt, who was the Prime Minister of England. The city is often referred to as the "City of Champions" due to the success of its professional sports teams.

Plad, MO - The town's name was designated to be known as "Glad". The Post Office made a clerical error and named the town "Plad". The local community decided that it was too hard to fight the government and accepted the name.

Plainville, KS - The town is properly named. The community is located in the Paradise Flats of Kansas. This is a long stretch of plain. Plainville is known as the "Windmill City". The wind really blows in this part of the country and the city has many windmills that are used to pump water.

Plano, TX - The origin of this name comes from the Spanish word meaning "plain" or "level".

Platte City & Plattsburg, MO - Both towns were named from the 1836 Platte Purchase. Platte is a word from the Dutch and Indian word meaning "flat" or level.

Plymouth, MA - It is probably the oldest town in the United States. The Pilgrims came here in 1620 on the "Mayflower". They named their town after Plymouth, England.

Pontiac, MI - The city was named to honor the chief of the Ottawa Indians. Chief Pontiac led a rebellion against British rule. He was later murdered by his enemy, a Peoria Indian.

Poplar Bluff, MO - The town got its name from the beautiful poplar trees on a bluff overlooking the Black River. In 1855, the first court house was erected. In 1870, the town was incorporated.

Portland, ME - Legend has it that the city's name was decided by a toss of a coin to end a dispute.

Portland, OR - The city was named after the city of Portland, Maine. Portland, Oregon is considered the "City of Roses". The Portland Rose Society was formed in 1888. Their first rose show started in 1889 and continues annually through today.

Potlatch, ID - The origin of the name has nothing to do with cooking. It comes from a Chinook Indian term meaning "springtime ceremonial gathering".

Potosi, MO - The land was originally acquired from a Spanish grant. Mining was very popular in the area. It is believed that the town was named after a famous mining town in Mexico that flourished during the late 1700's.

Poughkeepsie, NY - The community gets its name from an Algonquin Indian term meaning "waterfall" or "pleasant harbor".

Pretty Prairie, KS - Mary Collingwood came to Kansas in 1872. She was a widow and brought her nine children and two wagons from Crawford County, Indiana. When she reached the level ground with no rocks or trees she commented "what a pretty prairie". She chose this name when her home became a stagecoach stop.

Princeton, MO - The community was settled in 1846. The town was named in honor of the "Battle of Princeton" during the Revolutionary War. Martha Jane Canary grew up here. She was later known as "Calamity" Jane. She made history when she headed west!

Protem, MO - After the Civil War, Union Captain Christopher Columbus established a post office in this area. He had trouble choosing a name that wasn't already taken. The Post Office suggested "protem". Protem is the Latin word for "temporary". The name lasted.

Providence, RI - The community was named in gratitude for "God's merciful providence". Providence is the capital of Rhode Island.

Provo, UT - The city was named in honor of an early French explorer. His name was Etienne Proveau. In 1849, the Mormons established a community here. It is the home of Brigham Young University.

Punxsutawney, PA - Yes, this is groundhog country but let's get to the legend of this town. The town's name comes from an old Indian legend. Supposedly, an evil Indian sorcerer appeared and killed the people coming from the East. Later, a young Indian chief killed the sorcerer and his body was burned to destroy the evil medicine. A swarm of sand flies emerged after this event and plagued the Indians. The Indians named this area "Ponksaduteney" meaning "town of the sand flies". Through mispronunciation and poor spelling the name "Punxsutawney" emerged. Now, let's get to the groundhog story. The Delaware Indians believed the creation of man happened here. They believed their forefathers were animals who evolved into humans. The first to cross the bridge into human form was "Wojak". The name "wojak" translates into "woodchuck". The area was full of these little critters and on February 2, 1886, the local newspaper declared it "Groundhog Day". The weather forecasting of the groundhog comes from a Dutch legend. Later, W.O. Smith, owner of the local newspaper and a U.S. Congressman, kept the event alive. Through radio and television, the town and the event has become famous throughout the world!

Qulin, MO - It was first known as Melville. When a post office was opened, it was found that the name was already taken. Legend has it that a man named it Qulin. The name was formed by using the first initials of his five daughters.

Rabbit Hash, KY - The name came into existence in 1847. A huge flood ravished the settlement during this time. A large rabbit population retreated into this area from the rising waters and became the main food source for the citizens. There were so many rabbits that the local people created a special stew called "hash". The dish became so popular that the community adopted the name of "Rabbit Hash". The town was completely submerged in 1937 by another flood. Today, only the Rabbit Hash General Store stands in this community. I'm not sure about the rabbit population!

Raleigh, NC - The town was named in honor of Sir Walter Raleigh. Sir Walter was famous for laying his coat across a puddle of water for a lady to walk to dry land. Raleigh is the capital of North Carolina and the second largest city in North Carolina.

Raytown, MO - Around 1850, William Ray was a blacksmith from Ohio who opened a shop in this area. His blacksmith shop became a landmark between Kansas City and Independence. When the town began, the neighbors around the area referred to it as Ray's town. The name caught on and later became known as Raytown.

Red Lick, TX - Sometime in the 1860's, this area became a town. The early settlers named it Red Lick referring to a red clay hill that had a salt lick.

Reno, NV - The community was named in honor of a Union General, Jesse Lee Reno. The general was killed in the Civil War. Reno is known as "The Biggest Little City in the World".

Richmond, VA - This city was originally named after the town in England. It was established in 1737 by William Bryd II.

Riddle, OR - This name isn't a joke. Around 1851, the community was named for William H. Riddle. Riddle was a pioneer from Springfield, IL.

Ringgold, GA - The town was incorporated in 1847 and was named after Major Sam Ringgold. In 1846, the Major was fatally wounded in the Mexican War. He was the first officer to die in the Mexican War.

Rochester, NY - The city was named in honor of Colonel Nathaniel Rochester, an early settler. He laid out the town in 1811. Rochester was a well known soldier who fought in the Revolutionary War.

Rogers, AR - In 1881, the Frisco Railroad decided to blaze their tracks through this area. The railroad was building a route from St. Louis to San Francisco. The town was named in honor of C.W. Rogers. Rogers was the Vice President and General Manager of the Frisco Railroad.

Rolla, MO - The best legend for the origin of this name comes from early settlers. The settlers were from Carolina and very homesick for the people they left behind. They wanted to name their new town after their hometown of Raleigh, North Carolina. Through poor spelling and grammar, the pronunciation of the town's name evolved into "Rolla" instead of Raleigh.

Russell, KS - Both the county and the town of Russell were named for Avra P. Russell. He was only 28 when the Civil War broke out. He helped form the Second Kansas Infantry. He was elected First Lieutenant and rose to Captain under President Lincoln. The town was settled around 1871. Russell is the hometown of Senator Bob Dole. The community is known for its post rock.

Sacramento, CA - The city's name is a variation from a Spanish term meaning "holy sacrament".

Saddle Rock, NY - This area was settled in the early 1700's by "Mad Nan", a woman who tried to force out the Mattinecock Indians. The town's name comes from a local landmark. There was a large rock in the shape of a saddle. Early map makers referred to this area as "Saddle Rock". A grist mill operated here and a settlement was established. The town was later incorporated around 1910.

Salt Lake City, UT - The city was founded by members of The Church of Jesus Christ of Latter-Day Saints (Mormons). They chose the name after the great lake in Utah which is very salty.

San Diego, CA - Originally settled by the Spanish, the city is named after St. James, the Apostle.

Sandwich, NH - The community was named in honor of the Earl of Sandwich who was John Montagu.

San Francisco, CA - The city's name is Spanish for St. Francis of Assisi.

San Jose, CA - The city's name is Spanish for St. Joseph. The community was founded in 1777. San Jose was the first civilian settlement in California.

Santa Claus, IN - On Christmas Eve in 1849, the citizens of the community had a town meeting to decide the new name of the town. During the meeting, someone dressed as Santa Claus showed up with a bag of presents. The citizens wanted to name their new town "Santa Fe" but the name was already taken. Someone in the crowd suggested the name "Santa Claus" and the holiday spirit of that night led everyone to agree! In 1856, the Post Office agreed with the name of "Santa Claus".

Santa Fe, NM - Founded in 1609, the city's name is a Spanish derivative meaning "holy faith". Spanish explorers made it a capital city in 1607. This event makes Santa Fe the oldest capital of the United States. Officially, Santa Fe became the capital of New Mexico in 1912.

Savage, MN - The name has nothing to do with being a hostile place to live. It was named in honor of Marion Savage, a famous horse breeder in the area. Mr. Savage owned the great race horse, Dan Patch. Dan Patch was never defeated in any of his races. Savage was a great promoter and the horse became a legend. But in 1916, Dan Patch's heart stopped suddenly and the horse died. Thirty two hours later after his favorite horse had expired, Marion Savage died from a heart attack.

Savannah, GA - The early settlers came up with this name from an Indian term. The Indian term means "grassy plain". General James Oglethorpe founded the city around 1733.

Schenectady, NY - The area was first inhabited by the Mohawk Indians. Dutch settlers arrived in 1661. The Mohawks later called the settlement "Schaunaughtada". This term means "over the pine plains". The Dutch later shortened this name to "Schenectady" and changed the meaning. Their new word "Schenectady" now meant "bend in the Mohawk River". The community was once known as "The City that Lights and Hauls the World". It was once the home of the Edison Electric Company and the American Locomotive Company.

Seattle, WA - The name was chosen in honor of an Indian chief. The chief was leader of the Puget

Indians and was best known for his ability to negotiate treaties.

Secretary, MD - Sorry, this town was not named for any lady secretaries. The origin of this name comes from a much earlier time. It was named in honor of Henry Sewell who was the Secretary of the Colony under Governor Charles Calvert.

Sedalia, MO - The community was named after the founder's daughter Sarah "Sed" Smith. Sedalia was the birthplace of famous ragtime musician, Scott Joplin.

Shickshinny, PA - The origin of this name is from an Indian term meaning "five mountains".

Show Low, AZ - Legend has it that two brothers living here always settled their disagreements with a card game. The winner was the one showing the low card.

Sibley, MO - In 1836, the settlement was established by Archibald Gamble. He named it Sibley in honor of George C. Sibley. Sibley was Archibald's brother-in-law and a trading agent for the fort nearby.

Sikeston, MO - This city was founded in 1860 by John Sikes. He was very instrumental in getting the railroad here when a route was being forged between

St. Louis and New Orleans. Sikes was successful and a town started to flourish at this site. The town was named in his honor.

Silver Plume, CO - The city was named after the Silver Plume Mine that was in the area. The mine company was named for the plumes of silver found in the hills that looked like feathers. The town once flourished in the 1800's.

Sleepy Eye, MN - The city was named in honor of Chief Sleepy Eye. He was a Dakota Chief that was peaceful and agreed on many treaties with the U.S. Government and settlers coming to the area.

Smackover, AR - The town was named after the Smackover River. Originally, the French named the river "Sumac Couvert" meaning "covered with sumac". Through the years of poor spelling and mispronunciations the word evolved into "Smackover". This is quite an extraordinary translation from the French to the Arkansas version!

Smithville, MO - In 1824, Humphrey and Nancy Smith from New York moved to this area. They built a powered mill on the river. Smith frequently was called "Yankee Smith" by the southern sympathizers in the area.

Snowflake, AZ - It is not known to snow a lot in Arizona. The origin of this name comes from its founders, Apostle Erastus Snow and William Flake. Snow was a promoter of the Mormon faith and Flake was a Mormon land agent.

Social Circle, GA - It is believed that the community was named "Social Circle" because it was a popular resting spot for many travelers on their way to the western frontier.

Sopchoppy, FL - The name of this town comes from an Indian term meaning "red oak". The area hosts the "Worm Grunting Festival" every year.

Spokane, WA - Some say this city was named in honor of an Indian chief. Others say the city got its name from an Indian term meaning "children of the sun". Spokane became a community in 1893.

Springfield, MA - The town's name comes from Springfield, England. It was founded by William Pynchon of the Massachusetts Colony. The city served as an arsenal during the Revolutionary War.

St. James, MO - In 1858, the son of Thomas James became the town's postmaster. He first named it Jamestown but the Post Office rejected the name because there were already a lot of other towns with similar names. It is believed that no saint was involved. The saint was added just to satisfy the Post Office.

St. Joseph, MO - The city was originally known as Robdioux's trading post. In 1843, the city was named in honor of Joseph Robdioux. The saint in St. Joseph is for the town's opinion of Robidioux and not for the patron saint, St. Joseph, of <u>The Bible</u>.

St. Louis, MO - In 1764, Pierre Laclede received a land grant from the King of France. He and his 13 year old scout Auguste Chouteau selected the site as a fur trading post. Laclede is credited with being the city's founder but the young Chouteau later went on to build the city. During this time, most of the settlers were French. The town was named in honor of the French King. The town gained fame and prospered after Lewis and Clark started their famous expedition here. St. Louis was incorporated in 1823. St. Louis is known for being the "Gateway to the West".

St. Paul, MN - The twin city was named after an early chapel in the area dedicated to St. Paul, the Apostle.

Steelville, MO - The town became a county seat in 1835 when James Steel sold his land to the county. The town was named in his honor and later became an industrious mining town.

Stockton, MO - The town was settled in 1846 and was named in honor of Commodore Robert F. Stockton. Commodore Stockton is credited with saving the State of California during the Mexican War.

Strawberry Point, IA - In 1841, the "Old Mission Road" was being laid out. The workers put stakes out and marked them every mile. At this point, they marked the stake "Strawberry Point". The town is noted for having the "Largest Strawberry in the World". However, the strawberry may not be real!

Stringtown, MO - The town was named for the way it was laid out. The town had a string of houses with a store at each end.

Sturgis, SD - The town was named in honor of Lt. Jack Sturgis. The lieutenant died along with General Custer at the "Battle of the Little Big Horn". Annually in August, the town has one of the largest and wildest motorcycle rallies in the United States.

Sugar Land, TX - Legend goes that Samuel M. Williams received land in the area from famous Texan, Stephen Austin. Williams knew a freight boat operator who brought him sugar cane plants from Cuba. Williams started a sugar mill here and the rest is history.

Surprise, AZ - In 1938, Homer C. Ludden founded the community. He was a politician and a real estate developer. He named his new town after his hometown in Nebraska. Legend has it that the settlers in Nebraska were *surprised* to find their land was rich for farming. Surprise, AZ is the winter home for the Kansas City Royals baseball team.

Suwanee, GA - The community was established in 1837. This area was named earlier for the Shawnee Indians who lived here. It is thought that the city's name was a mispronunciation of "Shawnee". Shawnee is an Indian word meaning "Southerner".

Sweet Springs, MO - In 1826, early settler John Yantiss named the site due to its springs. The town became a popular health spa in the 1870's. It became so popular that the prestigious Marmaduke family built a huge hotel resort in the area.

Sylacauga, AL - Fernando DeSoto explored this area in 1540. The name comes from a Muskogean Indian term meaning "buzzard roost". The town of Sylacauga received national attention in 1954 when a meteorite hit the community. The meteor crashed through the roof of Ms. Hodge's house. The meteor hit the floor and bounced up and struck Ms. Hodges who was lying on the couch! She survived the event but I don't know about the house!

Tacoma, WA - The origin of this name comes from the Indian word for Mount Rainier. Tacoma is known as the "City of Destiny".

Talladega, AL - This settlement started at the foothills near the Appalachian Mountains. The origin of the name comes from a Creek Indian word meaning "town on the border".

Tallahassee, FL - The town's name comes from a Muskogean Indian word meaning "old fields" or "old town". Tallahassee is the capital of Florida by default. State legislatures were in disagreement over Pensacola or St. Augustine becoming the capital. After much debate, the politicians decided on Tallahassee as the compromise.

Tampa, FL - First visited by Ponce de Leon in 1521, the settlement began after the establishment of Fort Brooke in 1832. A couple of translations of this name are "near" and "split wood".

Tempe, AZ - The community was named for the Vale of Tempe. This was a narrow valley in northern Greece.

Ten Sleep, WY - The community got its name from an Indian's measurement of distance. This area was ten sleeps away from Fort Laramie.

Theodosia, MO - Theodosia was really started in 1886 when Tully D. Kirby opened a post office here. He named the town after his daughter. Others say it was named after a previous postmaster who had twins by the names of Theodore and Dosia. Other accounts say there was another postmaster that named the town after his wife. Take your pick!

Tickfaw, LA - The origin of this name comes from an Indian term meaning "pine rest".

Tightwad, MO - Yes, there is a *tightwad* involved with this legend. A local store owner cheated a customer out of 50 cents. Early settlers and travelers coming to the area referred to this community as "Tightwad".

Titonka, IA - The town was originally known as Ripley but it was discovered that there was another town by that name. Captain Ingam suggested the name "Titonka" in memory of a successful buffalo hunt with his friends. The word "Titonka" was an Indian term meaning "buffalo hunt. It must have been quite a hunt. The event happened some 40 years earlier!

Toad Suck, AR - This name isn't a joke. The town's name comes from the early settlers. The river trade here drew many questionable characters to the area. Many of them *sucked* on their whiskey and swelled up like *toads*. Because of this behavior, the area became known as Toad Suck.

Toledo, OH - The community was named after the city in Spain. Toledo is the 4th largest city in Ohio.

Tombstone, AZ - Mining for gold and silver was popular here in the late 1800's. Prospector Ed Schieffelin was told he would only find his tombstone in the San Pedro Valley. Having found his silver here, Ed named his first silver claim Tombstone. Later, it became the name of the town. Incorporated in 1881, the town became famous for the legend of the OK Corral.

Tonganoxie, KS - The town was founded in 1854. It was named in honor of a famous chief that lived nearby. Chief Tonganoxie was the leader of the Delaware Indians.

Topeka, KS - In 1854, Cyrus Holliday, owner of the A. T. & Santa Fe Railroad, formed a town company with a group of investors. During a meeting to decide the new name for the town, F.W. Giles suggested the name "Topeka". After much discussion, the name was adopted. Topeka is an Indian name for "wild potato" which grew abundantly on the banks of the Kansas River.

Trenton, NJ - This area was first known as Trent's town. Its founder was William Trent. Trent built a lavish and imposing brick structure on his 300 acres of land. He also had a grist mill for grinding grain and a saw mill for producing lumber.

Trinidad, CO - There is a dispute over the origin of this name. Some say it comes from the Spanish word "trinity". Others say it was named for Trinidad Baca, a daughter of an early settler who lived in the area. Dr. Stanley Biber moved to this area in the 1960's. He started to perform sex change operations. Some say Trinidad is the "Sex Change Capital of the World". Most of the citizens do not agree!

Truth or Consequences, NM - The city was named after the radio game show in 1950 hosted by Ralph Edwards. Edwards announced that he would broadcast his show from the first town to change its name to Truth or Consequences. The citizens from this area agreed and Edwards and his show moved to the town. It was originally called Hot Springs.

Tuba City, AZ - The town was first settled by the Mormans around 1870. The name comes from a Hopi Indian word meaning "tangled waters". There doesn't seem to be any music story!

Tucson, AZ - The name "Tucson" is derived from the Spanish word "Papago". This word means "black base". The Papago was also an Indian tribe that lived in the area. The Spanish built a garrison here calling it Presidio San Augustin del Tuscon. In 1775, Tucson Presidio was established to protect the settlers from Apache Indian attacks. Mexico sold this territory to the United States in 1853.

Tucumcari, NM - The name comes from an *unbelievable* Indian legend riddled with tragedy. Chief Wautonomah of the Apache Indian tribe was close to death. The chief had to decide which of his two finest braves would succeed him as the new chief. The names of the two braves were Tonopah and Tocom. These two braves hated each other and both were in love with Kari, Chief Wautonomah's beautiful daughter. The chief decided that Tonopah and Tocom would battle each other with knives to decide who would become the new chief and win the hand of Kari. When the fight began, Kari, the young Indian maiden, was hiding to see which brave would survive the fight. Tonopah stabbed Tocom in the heart, mortally wounding the brave. Kari was truly in love with Tocom and ambushed Tonopah. She plunged her knife into Tonopah's heart and then took her own life. When Chief Wautonomah heard of this news, the chief plunged his daughter's knife into his own heart. As he died from his mortal wound he cried out, "Tocom-Kari". The area was known thereafter as "Tucumcari". Later, the word "tucumcari" was a term used by the Indians meaning "place of ambush".

Tulsa, OK - One version says it was named for a tribe of Creek Indians. Others say it was named for an old Creek town in Alabama.

Tupelo, MS - The town was named after the gum trees found in this region. The area was explored by DeSoto as early as 1540 but was not incorporated as a city until 1870. Tupelo is the birth place of Elvis Presley.

Tuscaloosa, AL - Hernando DeSoto first explored this area. He battled a fierce group of Indians led by Chief Black Warrior. When the town was incorporated in 1819, the settlers named their town in honor of this fierce chief. The name "Tuscaloosa" is a Choctaw term. The words "tushka" means "warrior" and "lusa" means "black". In 1831, the town became home to the University of Alabama.

Two Egg, FL - The legend says a father gave his two children each a chicken. The children came to town and traded their chickens' eggs for candy at the local store. Travelers and local residents hearing of these transactions called the place Two Egg Crossing. The name stuck and it later became known as just Two Egg.

Unalaska, AK - This is the 11th largest city in Alaska. The Aleut Indian term "alaska" means "great land". When you add the "un" the term becomes "this great land". The town is located in the heart of the Aleutian Islands. This beautiful area is *very* Alaska.

Valentine, NE - This town was named for E.K. Valentine who was a politician in Nebraska. He was instrumental for getting the federal government to listen to the farmers' grievances. The biggest day of the year in this town is still Valentine's Day.

Vidalia, GA - The community got its name from a daughter of the man who built the Savannah, Americus & Montgomery Railroad. The name was a contraction of "via dalia". It means "by the way of dahlias". The city is world renowned for its famous sweet Vidalia onions.

Virginia City, NV - The town was named in honor of prospector "Old Virginia" Fennimore. He arrived in the area around 1851. In 1859, gold and silver were discovered in the hills and Virginia City began to flourish.

Wakeeney, KS - Albert Warren and James Keeney were co-owners of the Chicago Land Company. They planned a community here when the Kansas Pacific Railroad came through the area. Their two names were combined to form the town's name.

Walla Walla, WA - The community is named after an Indian tribe. This Indian term means "little river" or "many waters".

Warrensburg, MO - Martin Warren was a blacksmith by trade. Prairie residents would often stop for services and information at his place. Over time, it was referred to as Warren's corner and eventually became known as Warrensburg.

Warsaw, MO - In 1837, the town was named after the capital of Poland. Warsaw was chosen in honor of a Polish patriot who fought with General Nathanial Greene in the Revolutionary War. His name was Tadeusz Kosciuszko.

Waterloo, IA - The city was named after the town in Belgium and the "Battle of Waterloo". The Belgium town is where Napoleon was finally defeated by the British.

Waverly, IA - The town was named after the first novel written by Sir Walter Scott. Sir Walter's novel Waverly was published in 1814. Shortly after, he published the "Waverly novels", which were about romances of Scottish life. Sir Walter is considered the father of historic novels. He was very famous during the 1800's but died in bankruptcy. However, his books became so popular that Sir Walter was able to pay his debts off from his grave.

Weed, CA - The community is located in a *beautiful* area situated near the Oregon border. The town was named in honor of its founder, Abner Weed.

Weeki Wachee, FL - The name is a Muskogean Indian term meaning "little spring".

Welcome, NC - The name was chosen over a dispute on what to call the new railroad depot.

Wichita, KS - The name "Wichita" comes from the Wichita Indians who settled in this area. The word "Wichita" means "painted faces" or "scattered lodges". One hundred twenty three men and one woman incorporated the town in 1871. The one woman, Mrs. Catherine McCarthy, had a son by the name of Henry. Henry later changed his name to William Bonney, better known as "Billy the Kid"!

Winnemucca, NV - This area was established by local beaver trappers. The wagon trains traveling through stopped here because of the trading post that was on the trail. The town was named in honor of Chief Winnemucca, a Paiute Indian who lived in this area.

Winston-Salem, NC - The city was named in honor of Major Joseph Winston, a Revolutionary War hero. The major fought many battles against the Cherokee

Indians and the British. It merged with the town of Salem in 1913.

Woonsocket, RI - The town was named after an Indian term meaning "thunder mist". It's hard to believe but there are two Woonsocket's in the United States. This town is the original one. The community was established here in 1888. The other Woonsocket is in South Dakota. A railroad official that was constructing a new track in South Dakota used the same name. The railroad official named the South Dakota town after his hometown in Rhode Island.

Wynot, NE - Legend has it that when selecting a name for this town, an elderly gentleman suggested the name "Why Not"? Other accounts say the name comes from the Wynota Indians.

Yazoo City, MI - It is a strange name but it comes from the Indians. It was named after the tribe of Yazoo Indians that lived in the area.

Yellville, AR - The town was founded in 1835. It was named in honor of Arkansas Governor Archibald Yell. Governor Yell fought in the War of 1812. After the war, he became a federal judge and congressman. The town is now known for the annual "National Wild Turkey Calling Contest".

Yonkers, NY - The landowner of this community was a Dutchman by the name of Jonkeer Van Donck. It is believed that the Dutch term "Jonkeers" means "young lords".

Zap, ND - The community was named in honor of a town in Scotland.

Zebulon, NC - The community was named after Zebulon B. Vance. He was a governor and U.S. Senator. The town came into existence when the Raleigh & Pamlico Sound Railroad built a track through this area. Zebulon is home to the Carolina Mud Cats minor league baseball team.

Zelienople, PA - The town was established in 1807 by Baron Demar Basse. In 1802, the Baron purchased over 10,000 acres of land in the western part of Pennsylvania. He named his new town after his eldest daughter. Her name was "Zelienople"!

II. Names of the 50 States

Alabama - The name comes from a southern tribe of Indians. It was spelled various ways by the Spanish, French and British settlers to the area. Translated the name "alba" means "a thick or mass of vegetation" and "amo" translates "to clear, to collect or gather up".

Alaska - The name is an Indian Aleut word that means "great land". In 1867, the United States purchased Alaska from Russia for 7.2 million dollars. At the time, most Americans thought it was a waste of money. In 1959, Alaska became the 49th state of the Union. The region is rich in resources.

Arizona - Charles D. Poston, a mining speculator, first suggested the name "Arizona" in a petition to the United States Congress to make Arizona a legal territory. The name comes from the Papago Indians. The Papago words "aleh" and "zon" mean "little spring". The name "Arizona" was chosen for the state because it sounded better than the other suggestions which were Pimeria and Gadsonia.

Arkansas - The name "Arkansas" comes from the Quapaw Indians, by way of early French explorers. The term means "people living downstream". These Native Americans were also called the Arkansaw. This name was used for the land where these Native Americans lived.

California - The legend has it that the name California comes from a sixteenth century novel. Garcia Ordonez wrote a popular novel in this time called <u>Las Sergas de Esplandiandonez de Montalvo</u>. Hernando Cortez was familiar with this book and probably named the territory after the gold enriched island described in the novel.

Colorado - Mining lobbyist, George M. Willing first presented the name to Congress. He told Congress that "Idaho" was a Shoshone word that meant "gem of the mountains". Congress was about to name the region "Idaho" until they found out that it was just a name that Mr. Willing had made up. Congress then decided on the name "Colorado". This name was Spanish for the color "red" which refers to the color of water found in the Colorado River.

Connecticut - Thomas Hooker founded the area in 1636. The colony was named after an Algonquin Indian word, "quinnehtukqut". It means "beside the long tidal river". It became a state in 1788.

Delaware - Peter Minuit founded this colony in 1638. It was named for the Delaware Indians. Some suggest that the name was to honor an early colonial governor, Lord de la Warr. Delaware became a state in 1787.

Florida - The peninsula was named by Ponce de Leon who came here in 1513. The Spanish words "pascua florida" mean "flowery easter".

Georgia - James Oglethorpe founded the region and named it after England's King George II. It became a state in 1788.

Hawaii - In 1778, Captain James Cook first called the islands, the "Sandwich Islands" in honor of the Earl of Sandwich. However, King Kamehameha I united the islands under his rule by 1819 and called his kingdom "Hawaii". The name "Hawaii" has two origins. The first part of the word "haw" means "traditional homeland" and the second part of the word "ii" means "small and raging". Another account of its origin is that the name comes from the true founder of the islands, Hawaii Loa.

Idaho - George M. Willing, a well known mining lobbyist in Washington, D.C., made up the name "Idaho". He claimed it was a Shoshone word meaning "gem of the mountains". Gold had just been discovered in this region and the area became known as the "Idaho Mines". There was also a major steamboat used in the gold rush up the Columbia River known as the "Idaho". The name became well known around the country and Congress decided to use the name for the new state.

Illinois - The state gets its name from Indian tribes. In the mid 1600's, the Illinois Indians were a large group of tribes sharing the same language and culture. At one time, there were over 25,000 Indians. They were eventually driven into Oklahoma.

Indiana - Indiana was created from the Northwest Territory in 1800. The name means "land of Indians." It became a state in 1816.

Iowa - The state of Iowa was named after the Iowa River. The Iowa River was named after the Iowa Indians who lived in this territory. The tribal name "Ayuxwa" was spelled by the French as "Ayoua" and by the English as "Iowa". The word "Iowa" means "one who puts to sleep".

Kansas - This state gets its name from the Kansa or Kanza Indian tribe. The Kansa were native to northeast Kansas when the first white explorers arrived. They made treaties with the white settlers but were eventually driven into Oklahoma in 1873.

Kentucky - The name's origin was once believed to come from a Native American word meaning "dark and bloody hunting ground". Later, it was attributed to the meaning "land of tomorrow" or "cane and turkey lands" or "meadow lands". The last legendary answer suggests that the name comes from a Shawnee Indian town named Eskippathiki.

Louisiana - Robert Cavelier Sieur de La Salle was the first to really explore the Mississippi River Delta. He named the area in 1682, "La Louisianne" in honor of his king, Louis XIV of France. Louisiana is the English form of this word.

Maine - It is uncertain how the name for this state originated. One account suggests that the state was named by French colonists after the French province of Mayne. Another theory mentions that the word "main" was a common term used to describe a mainland.

Maryland - This area was founded in 1633 by Lord Baltimore. While having a conversation with King Charles, the King wanted to name the new region after his wife. It was decided to name the new area Maryland. The King's wife was Queen Henrietta Maria of England. Maryland thrived but King Charles I was later beheaded for treason. Maryland became a state in 1788.

Massachusetts - John Winthrop founded the region in 1630. The colony was named after the Massachusetts Indians. The word "massachusetts" means "large hill". Massachusetts became a state in 1788.

Michigan - The name "Michigan" comes from the Indian word "michigama" meaning "great" or "big lake". The French first used the word to describe

Lake Michigan. It was first used officially to refer to this land when Congress created the Territory of Michigan in 1805.

Minnesota - The state gets its name from an Indian term meaning "cloudy water". Minnesota has over 12,000 lakes. Over 91 lakes are named "Long Lake". Let's hope we never have to meet a friend at Long Lake!

Mississippi - The Indians named the big river the "Mississippi". French explorer La Salle used the name on his map in 1695. The state was named after the river.

Missouri - This state's name comes from a tribe of Sioux Indians called the Missouris. The name "Missouri" often has been construed to mean "muddy water" but the official interpretation of the name stands for town of the large canoes". Other authorities have said the Indian syllables come from a word that means "wooden canoe people" or "he of the big canoe". Most people that reside in this state pronounce their state's name as "Mis-sour-rah". I guess no one wants to live in *misery*!

Montana - Montana was created out of the Idaho Territory in 1864. The name was created from the Latin word "montaanus" which means mountainous. Helena became the capital under a huge scandal in

1894. Copper king, William Clark spent millions of dollars in bribes and buying votes to get his town Helena designated as the capital.

Nebraska - The name comes from the Platte River. The Omaha Indians called this river "Iboapka" meaning "broad river". The name "Nebraska" was used by influential politician John C. Fremont when describing the Platte River in this area. In 1854, Congress used the term "Nebraska" to name the new territory.

New Hampshire - Richard Wheelwright founded the colony. It was named after the County of Hampshire in England. It became a state in 1788.

New Jersey - The English colonists are credited for settling this area in 1664. The colony was named for the Isle of Jersey in England. It became a state in 1787.

New Mexico - The name of this state comes from the Spanish words "Nuevo Mexico". The name was used to describe the upper Rio Grande region. The word "Mexico" is an Aztec term meaning "place of Mexitli". Mexitli was one of the Aztec gods.

New York - Peter Minuit also founded this colony in 1626. It was named after the Duke of York. New York became a state in 1788.

Nevada - Nevada was named after the mountains the early Spaniards called the "Sierra Nevadas".

North & South Carolina - Virginia colonists migrated south and found this region in 1653. The colony was named from a derivative of "Carolus", the Latin word for "Charles" who was the English King at the time. Ten years after North Carolina was established, English colonists went south and used the same name.

North & South Dakota - Dakota was the name used for this region. Both North and South Dakota were one territory until 1889. Dakota is the Sioux word for "allies" or "friends".

Ohio - The origin of the name comes from an Iroquois Indian term meaning "large" or "beautiful river". The state was named after the river.

Oklahoma - The name "Oklahoma" comes from the language of the Choctaw people, who were removed from Mississippi to the area of Oklahoma. Oklahoma is a combination of two Choctaw words, "okla" meaning "people", and "homa" meaning "red". Translated, the state is home to the red people, the Indians. The name was suggested by Allen Wright, Chief of the Choctaw Nation from 1866 to 1870.

Oregon - The name "Oregon" is from a French-Canadian term "ouragan". The meaning of this term is "squall" or "storm".

Pennsylvania - William Penn was its founder. The region was named after Penn and the Latin word meaning "forest". It became a state in 1787.

Rhode Island - Roger Williams founded this area in 1636. The origin of the name is from the Dutch words meaning "red island". It became a state in 1790.

Tennessee - The first account of this name comes from a Spanish explorer named Captain Juan Pardo. He encountered an Indian village by the name of Tanasqui. The meaning and origin of the name is uncertain. Other accounts believe the name Tennessee is a modification of a Cherokee term meaning "meeting place", "winding river" or "river of the great bend". Later, James Glen, Governor of South Carolina gave the modern day spelling of Tennessee from his correspondence during the 1750's.

Texas - Even though the state evolved from the country of Mexico it is not a Spanish name. The name "Texas" comes from the language of the Caddo Indian tribes. The Spanish explorers and settlers used this word to refer to the friendly Indian tribes throughout Louisiana, Oklahoma and Texas. The original word "teysha" means "hello friend".

Utah - The Navajo Indians were referred to by the Apache as the Yuttahih. This means "one that is further north". The early settlers misunderstood this term and the tribes in this area were referred to as the Utes or the Utahs. The land of the Utes later became the land of Utah.

Vermont - In 1647, French explorer Samuel de Champlain called the region "Verd Mont". This was a French term meaning "green mountain". Vermont is the English form of the name.

Virginia - The state was founded in 1607 by John Smith at Jamestown. The colony was named after the "Virgin Queen", Elizabeth I. Virginia became a state in 1788.

Washington - This is not a hard one to figure out. In 1853, the Washington Territory was established and named in honor of the first President of the United States, George Washington.

West Virginia - Originally this area was part of Virginia. It was named in honor of Queen Elizabeth I the "Virgin Queen". The region separated from Virginia and became a state in 1861.

Wisconsin - Wisconsin received its name from the Wisconsin River. The name "Wisconsin" comes from a French version of an Ojibwa Indian term. It is believed the name means "gathering of the waters" or "place of the beaver".

Wyoming - The name "Wyoming" is an Indian name meaning "at the big flats" or "large plains". This area was originally part of the Dakota Territory.